DATE DUE	

Inside Special Operations

GREEN BERETS

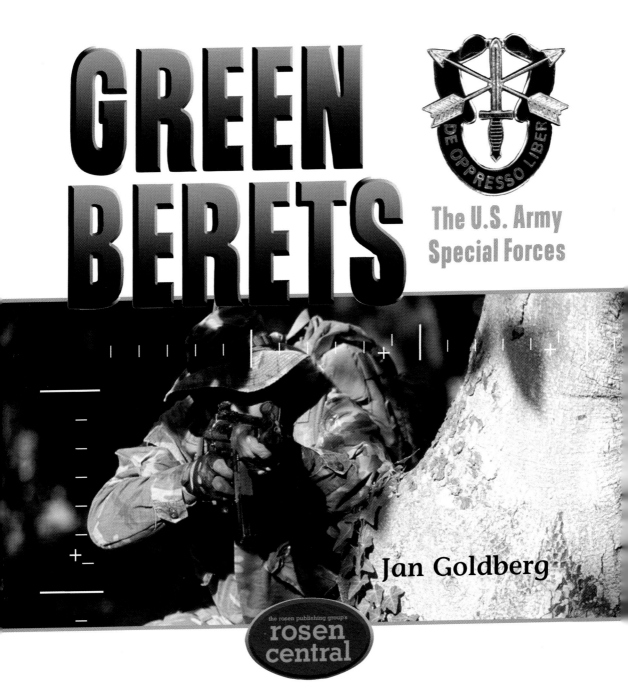

The U.S. Army Special Forces

Jan Goldberg

the rosen publishing group's
rosen
central

Published in 2003 by The Rosen Publishing Group, Inc.
29 East 21st Street, New York, NY 10010

Library of Congress Cataloging-in-Publication Data

Goldberg, Jan.
Green Berets : the U.S. Army Special Forces/by Jan Goldberg—1st ed.
  p. cm.—(Inside special operations)
Summary: A look at the Special Forces, better known as the Green Berets including their purpose, history, missions, requirements, training, and equipment.
Includes bibliographical references and index.
ISBN 0-8239-3808-5 (library binding)
1. United States. Army. Special Forces—Juvenile literature. [1.United States. Army. Special Forces. 2. Special forces (Military science)] I. Title. II. Series.
UA34.S64 G65 2002
356'.1673'0973—dc21

2002008485

Manufactured in the United States of America

Contents

Green Beret soldiers leave their MH-47 helicopter for a search operation in the southern Philippines.

Introduction

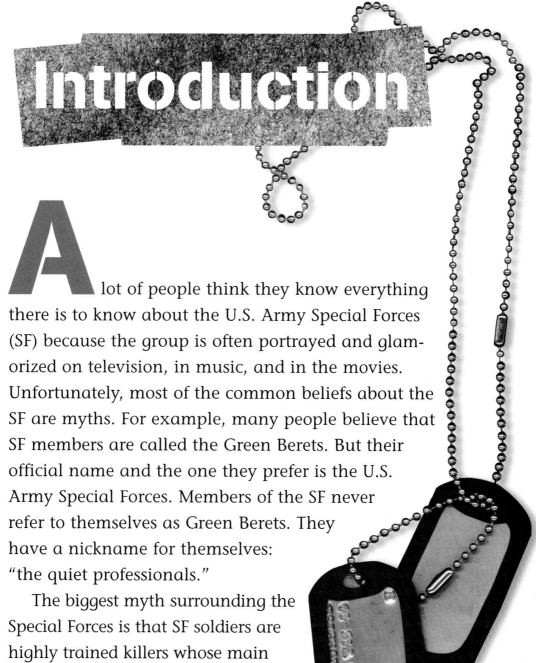

A lot of people think they know everything there is to know about the U.S. Army Special Forces (SF) because the group is often portrayed and glamorized on television, in music, and in the movies. Unfortunately, most of the common beliefs about the SF are myths. For example, many people believe that SF members are called the Green Berets. But their official name and the one they prefer is the U.S. Army Special Forces. Members of the SF never refer to themselves as Green Berets. They have a nickname for themselves: "the quiet professionals."

The biggest myth surrounding the Special Forces is that SF soldiers are highly trained killers whose main mission is to wipe out large groups of enemies. In movies like *Rambo* and television shows like *The A-Team*, SF soldiers are shown to be large, dangerous-looking men with bulging muscles. These men act as though they love to go to war. They can't wait for the shooting to start because they want a chance to show off. They're portrayed as young rebels who enjoy breaking the rules.

Real SF members must be in good physical shape, of course. But it's just as important—and maybe even more important—for SF members to be in good mental shape. They must be intelligent and mature, with good problem-solving skills and excellent people skills. They're not fresh out of school, either. Most SF members are in their thirties, with five to ten years of military experience behind them. SF members don't break the rules. In fact, the success of their missions usually depends on following the rules exactly. And, instead of loudly showing off, their goal is to blend quietly into their surroundings.

Most important, the main missions of the SF do not have anything at all to do with violent gun battles. As you will read later, SF members are teachers first and warriors second. SF soldiers don't want to fight the enemy unless they're forced to. They would much rather try to outsmart their enemies than shoot at them. This book will teach you about the U.S. Army Special Forces—the truth, not the myths.

1. How the Special Forces Began

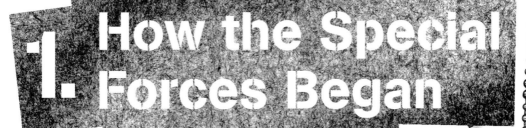

Many armies around the world have specialized units, or groups. These groups are trained to handle the military's most dangerous and difficult missions. In India, they are called the Para Commando Brigade. In South Africa, they're called the Special Forces Brigade. Britain calls them the Special Operations Group (SOG). One branch of Britain's SOG is called the Special Boat Service.

In the United States, special operations units are all part of the Special Operations Forces (SOF). The U.S. Special Operations Command

(SOCOM) is responsible for the training of the SOF. SOCOM's headquarters are at MacDill Air Force Base in Tampa, Florida. SOCOM is one of nine unified commands in the U.S. military.

The three best-known SOF units are the Navy SEALs, the Army Rangers, and the Army Special Forces (SF), what we commonly call Green Berets. SEAL stands for SEa-Air-Land. SEALs handle many different types of missions, but they are best known for their underwater skills. The Rangers' main missions involve direct action against the enemy. They rely heavily on their weapons during raids and attacks. The Rangers are the group that people most often confuse with the SF.

In 1942, the army formed the Office of Strategic Services, or the OSS. The OSS was responsible for sabotage and espionage during World War II. Several smaller groups were formed to carry out various missions. Some went deep into enemy territory to destroy roads, railroads, and bridges. Some patrolled the borders of foreign countries to keep the enemy from getting in. Others learned how to train the natives in those countries. They taught them how to fight the enemy themselves.

After World War II, the army realized that these types of specialized groups would always be needed. So, on June 20, 1952, the first official Special Forces group was formed. The unit was called the 10th Special Forces Group (Airborne). Based at Fort Bragg, North Carolina, this group was commanded by Colonel Aaron Bank.

U.S. Special Forces continued training after World War II, even though the United States was not involved in any wars. Above, soldiers learn how to operate a German machine gun at the U.S. Army Special Forces training course in Fort Bragg, North Carolina.

Current Special Forces Groups

As of early 2002, the United States had five active SF groups. Two are stationed at Fort Bragg. The others are stationed at Fort Lewis, Washington; Fort Campbell, Kentucky; and Fort Carson, Colorado. There are also some Army National Guard SF groups and Army Reserve SF groups. The men in these groups are called into active duty during a time of war or other emergency.

Each active SF group is responsible for a different part of the world. This is so its members can become experts about their assigned area. They learn the languages that are spoken in their area's countries. They also learn all they can about the people and the culture. It can take two years or more to learn certain foreign languages, so it makes sense that each group concentrates on a particular region of the world. No one would want to spend years learning Russian if he was going to be sent on a mission to South America.

Each SF group has a headquarters and three separate battalions. Each battalion has a headquarters plus three separate companies. Each company has its own headquarters, too, plus five or six operational teams. These teams are called Operational Detachment Alpha, or ODA. They are often called A teams or A detachments. The companies they are part of are called B detachments. The battalions are called C detachments. So each SF group has three C detachments (battalions), nine B detachments (companies), and forty-five or more A detachments (teams).

The A Team

An A team is usually made up of twelve men—two commissioned officers and ten enlisted men. Commissioned officers are soldiers who entered the army after graduating from college.

They are trained to be leaders. Enlisted men usually join the army after high school. Sometimes, enlisted men work their way up and become noncommissioned officers.

The two officers on the team serve as the captain and assistant commander. The enlisted soldiers on their team are all trained in certain specialty areas. There are five specialty areas. Two men on each team are experts in the same specialty.

Here is a list of all the different positions on an A team, with descriptions of their jobs. The number after each position is an MOS code. MOS stands for Military Occupational Specialty. All of the positions in the military have MOS codes.

ODA Commander (18A) Each A team has one lead captain. He is in charge of everything the team does. During training, 18As concentrate on mission planning, guerrilla warfare, and leadership skills.

Assistant Detachment Commander (180A) The assistant detachment commander is the second in command of the team. If something happens to the captain, the 180A can step in and take his place. For certain missions, a team might split into two equal parts. In this case, the 18A and the 180A can each command half the team.

Weapons Specialist (18B) Weapons specialists learn about all different types of weapons from all over the world. They know

A weapons specialist cleans and inspects a gun in preparation for a mission in Afghanistan. Weapons specialists must be experts on all aspects of all kinds of weaponry.

how to fire all the weapons and also how to clean, repair, and care for them. 18Bs are also excellent marksmen. This means that they are skilled enough to hit a very small target from very far away.

Demolitions/ Engineering Specialist (18C) These specialists know how to build and repair many different things, like roads, buildings, and bridges. They also know how to use explosives to blow up and destroy those same roads, buildings, and bridges. 18Cs might help a country build bridges during one mission. But they might try to destroy an enemy's headquarters during their very next mission.

Medical Specialist (18D) These specialists are like paramedics. 18Ds are specially trained to treat emergency wounds and injuries, like gunshot wounds and broken legs. They know how to perform emergency surgery and how to give medicines. But they can also treat snake and insect bites, pull teeth, test water sources, and help sick or injured animals.

Communications Specialist (18E) An A team must be able to communicate back to its base, no matter where it is in the world. 18Es can operate all types of communications devices. They can also repair radios, telephones, and other electronic equipment. They know all about the latest computer equipment, but they also know Morse code, a system used all over the world to relay messages over a radio or walkie-talkie. This system comes in very handy when a team is in a remote area without fancy communications equipment.

A Special Forces soldier uses his communication system to coordinate the evacuation of wounded soldiers. Communications specialists are important to the safety and success of an A team because they are responsible for reporting back to its base.

Operations/Intelligence Specialist (18F) These specialists know how to spy on the enemy. They've learned ways to get behind enemy lines without being noticed. They are trained in breaking codes and other secret communications. They are also expert photographers.

All of these specialists are important for the Special Forces' main type of mission, guerrilla warfare. Guerrilla warfare describes any type of irregular, or unconventional, fighting methods. Guerrillas aren't known for starting big gun battles. They seek to defeat the enemy in other ways, such as sabotage and surprise raids. They try to outsmart the enemy.

Before any of these specialists can operate in SF missions, they must each make it through intense training. The next chapter will teach you how SF members become the very best.

2. Special Forces Training

Because of the extreme dangers involved in Special Forces missions, the SF is an all-volunteer service. A candidate must decide for himself whether he wants to apply based upon all of the factors involved. He must take into consideration the fact that many SF missions require living in foreign countries for six months or more every year. He must realize that serving in the SF is hard on family life. Wives and children cannot travel with SF soldiers on their missions. Understandably, they can become very frustrated when they cannot see their husbands and fathers for long periods of time. The risks involved with being part of an SF team are also very hard for families to deal with. For these reasons, the divorce rate is very high among SF members.

Appropriate Candidates

Everyone applying for the SF must be male. This rule may change someday, but for now, Title 10 of the U.S. code says that women cannot serve on the military's front lines.

Men wanting to join the SF must be Airborne qualified, and they must earn a score of 206 or above on the Army Physical Fitness Test (APFT). They must also be strong swimmers and be in the best physical shape of their lives.

Beginning in January 2002, the army began a new recruitment program for the SF. They decided that men who were interested in serving in the SF could join from outside the military. Now, all ranks of soldiers can apply, but the requirements are a little different for each.

The Waiting Game

Once the above requirements are met, men interested in joining the SF are put on a list for the next opening at SFAS. SFAS stands for Special Forces Assessment and Selection. It is held at Colonel Nick Rowe Special Forces Training Facility at Camp MacKall, North Carolina, just west of Fort Bragg.

SF training takes at least a year to complete, and it usually takes longer. It is also very expensive, costing the army more than $100,000 per soldier. So, it's very important for the army to find out as soon as possible which men cannot handle the difficult training.

SFAS

SFAS is a twenty-four-day test to find out which men will move on to the next training phase. SFAS is so difficult that less than one-third of the men who start it are able to finish.

During SFAS, the men are put through tests similar to what they would face during a real SF mission. The instructors try not to get to know the students very well. They have to grade the students on whether they can handle the physical and mental challenges. Typically, by the second week of SFAS, at least half of the students will already have dropped out.

Here are just a few of the challenges that students face during SFAS:

Marches The students have to march two to five times every day, no matter what the weather is like. It might be blazing hot or it might be cold and snowy. The men are not told ahead of time how long the march will be. They just keep

Grueling SFAS tests help weed out recruits who aren't strong enough for the Special Forces. Special Forces soldiers must be in exceptional shape, both physically and mentally.

going until they are told to stop. During every march, they also carry loaded packs that can weigh fifty pounds (23 kilograms) or more.

Obstacle Course The obstacle course features many different types of obstacles, like walls, climbing ropes, and underground pipes. These obstacles test the students' physical abilities. But they are also a way for the instructors to find out if a student has any special problems. For example, a fear of heights or a fear of enclosed places are just two of the problems they look for. These types of fears could greatly affect the success of an SF mission.

Team Exercises SFAS is meant to test each student's individual abilities. But instructors also want to make sure that the students can work well together.

Situation and Reaction Students are given problems to solve. Often, they can use only the simple materials they are given or things found in nature. What makes this even more difficult is that the students are sleep-deprived because they don't get a lot of sleep during SFAS. They are often awakened during the middle of the night and sent on a long march. There is a reason for this. The instructors want to make sure the students can think clearly even when they are not well rested.

No one knows until the very end of SFAS whether or not he has passed. Those men who do not pass can either return to their original army service branch or go through SFAS again. The men who pass move on to the Special Forces Qualification Course (SFQC). SFQC is also called the Q Course. Much of the Q Course is also held at Camp MacKall in North Carolina.

The Q Course

The SFAS is simply a way to find out which men are good enough to move on to the Q Course. As you might expect, the Q Course is even more difficult than SFAS. This is where the army actually determines which men will make good SF soldiers.

The Q Course is broken up into three phases, and finishing it can take anywhere from eight months to more than a year. The time involved depends on which specialty training is followed during Phase II.

Phase I This phase is thirty-nine days long. Basic army skills are taught to every soldier. For more experienced soldiers, much of Phase I will be a review course. But by the end of the phase, every soldier will have the same level of knowledge. Many men still fail or drop out during this phase. But this time, the instructors do get to know all of the students personally. At this point, the job of the instructors is to help the students succeed.

Phase II During this phase, students follow one of eight separate courses. The course they take depends on which specialty they've chosen, or which they have been assigned to. Most of the courses last about six months. The course for medical sergeants is the longest, at twelve months. This course is run by the Special Operations Medical Training Battalion. This battalion also trains the medics from the other Special Operations Forces, like Rangers and Navy SEALs. Some of the medical training is also held in the emergency rooms of major hospitals in New York City and Tampa, Florida.

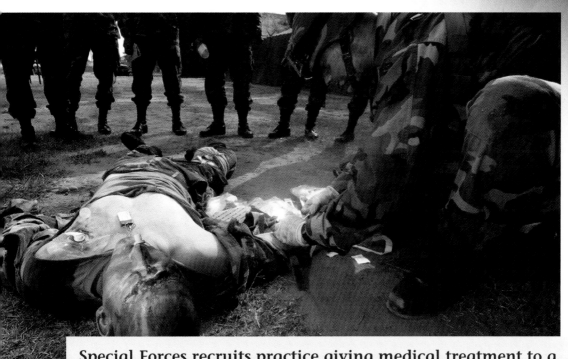

Special Forces recruits practice giving medical treatment to a soldier whose wounds were created with realistic makeup. Learning battlefield triage and first aid is important for all Special Forces operatives, but more specialized training is given to medical specialists.

Phase III This phase lasts thirty-eight days. It is the instructors' final chance to evaluate all the students. Because of the different training times in Phase II, students in Phase III are usually with a different group than they were with in Phase I. This is a good thing, though, because it helps the instructors tell whether the students can work successfully with different teams of people. It also shows them whether the students can adjust well to changes.

During Phase III, some review training takes place. For instance, on days four to six, students practice parachuting from airplanes and helicopters. Students are also taught some new skills during this phase. On days sixteen to twenty, for example, students learn about the SF practice of pre-mission isolation. Before going on a mission, a team of SF soldiers goes into an Isolation Facility (ISOFAC) to plan, train, and pack for their mission. The idea is to leave the team alone so that they can prepare for their mission in peace and quiet, without any interruptions.

Robin Sage, the Final Exam

Most of Phase III is spent preparing for a difficult final exam called Robin Sage. This is a field exercise that is meant to test everything the soldiers have learned. Of course, it tests what they've learned during the Q Course. But it also tests everything the soldiers have learned during their entire time in the army.

Robin Sage is extremely difficult. In fact, the problems given to the students seem almost impossible to solve. But the instructors make it this challenging for a very good reason. They feel that if the SF soldiers can pass Robin Sage, they will be able to handle just about anything that comes their way when they're on an SF mission.

Robin Sage takes place to the north and west of Camp MacKall and Fort Bragg. During the exercise, which takes place four times each year, this area is transformed into an imaginary foreign country called Pineland. The civilian people who live in this area let the army use their land at no charge. After Robin Sage is completed, members of the SF often spend time doing chores in the area, like mending fences and picking up litter. It's their way of expressing their thanks.

At the beginning of Robin Sage, the instructors divide the students into teams of twelve men each. Each team is assigned to a guerrilla group somewhere in the "country" of Pineland. The teams are then taken into Pineland. Most of them will have to parachute into Pineland from an airplane or helicopter. Once inside, the team must cache their equipment and supplies. Then they must find their assigned guerrilla group (called a G band) and begin organizing and training them.

Every team will meet many difficult challenges throughout the exercise. These challenges are meant to prepare them for a real SF mission. For instance, the transportation method might be changed at the last minute. They might have been told that they're parachuting into Pineland from a helicopter. But when they arrive at the takeoff spot the helicopter is not there, or it is broken down. Or the G Band they are assigned to might turn out to be hostile and unwilling to have SF soldiers try to train them. SF instructors and observers follow the teams every step of the way. They monitor the actions of the team, keep careful notes, and offer advice when necessary.

Robin Sage lasts fifteen days, taking place on days twenty-three to thirty-seven of Phase III. When it is completed, the soldiers are brought out of Pineland and taken back to the base. There, they turn in their equipment, write reports, and wait to hear if they have passed the Q Course. Those who have failed are sent to their next assignment. But those who have passed are given a night of rest. The next day, they are the guests of honor at an awards ceremony and dinner. Each Q Course graduate is presented with his Green Beret and a badge for this new SF group.

Language School

Though the men might have successfully passed the Q Course, their training is not over yet. Next comes language school. Soldiers must be able to speak the language of the country where they will be assigned. Every SF soldier learns at least one foreign language, but many have to learn more than one. It all depends on the area to which they have been assigned.

Some languages are also easier to learn than others. Those who speak English can learn Romance languages, like Spanish or French, pretty quickly. Speaking the language like a native might take only nine months or so. But some languages are much more difficult to learn. For example, becoming fluent in Chinese or Arabic can take two years or more.

The SERE Course

After language school, SF soldiers head back to Fort Bragg for SERE. This is Survival, Evasion, Resistance, and Escape school. In many ways, SERE is even more difficult than the Q Course. Most of what happens during SERE is highly classified. But SERE is meant to prepare SF soldiers for the possibility of being captured by the enemy during a mission. SERE tries to teach soldiers how to avoid becoming a prisoner of war. It also shows them how to survive if they are captured and how to find ways to escape. Many SF soldiers say that SERE is the very worst part of their SF careers.

Advanced Parachute Training

After SERE, it's time for advanced parachute training. This takes place at the Military Free-Fall Course at Yuma, Arizona. SF soldiers learn two major kinds of free-fall jumping. HALO means high altitude-low opening. During a HALO jump, soldiers jump from the aircraft at a high altitude. They don't open their parachutes right away, however. They free-fall for up to two minutes. During this time, they are falling at about 125 miles per hour. When they are only a few thousand feet above the ground, they open their chutes. During their free-fall, they cannot easily be picked up by enemy radar. HALO

jumps are especially effective during clandestine operations.

HAHO means high altitude-high opening. During a HAHO jump, soldiers open their parachutes right after they exit the aircraft. They can jump when they are outside the enemy border, then steer their parachutes into the enemy territory to land. HAHO jumps are also difficult to pick up on radar.

In advanced parachute training, a Special Forces recruit prepares to practice HALO (high altitude-low opening) jumps.

Combat Diver Certification Program

Following advanced parachute training, SF soldiers head to Key West, Florida, for a Combat Diver certification program. The Navy SEALs handle most of the military's underwater missions, but the SF also trains in this area. Soldiers learn the skills needed for different underwater breathing systems, like scuba (self-contained underwater breathing apparatus). They also learn how to navigate underwater.

Even though Navy SEALs are the Special Operations Force most associated with aquatic operations, Green Beret recruits must receive certification in combat diving. Here, trainees develop techniques in a U.S. Army Special Forces training camp swimming pool.

Trained and Ready!

The SF soldier's training is complete—for now. Over the next few years, SF soldiers can expect to spend at least six months out of every year downrange (overseas) and the rest of the time training. Once in a while, they might also find time for additional courses to sharpen their skills. Weapons specialists, for instance, might attend sniper school to practice their long-range shooting.

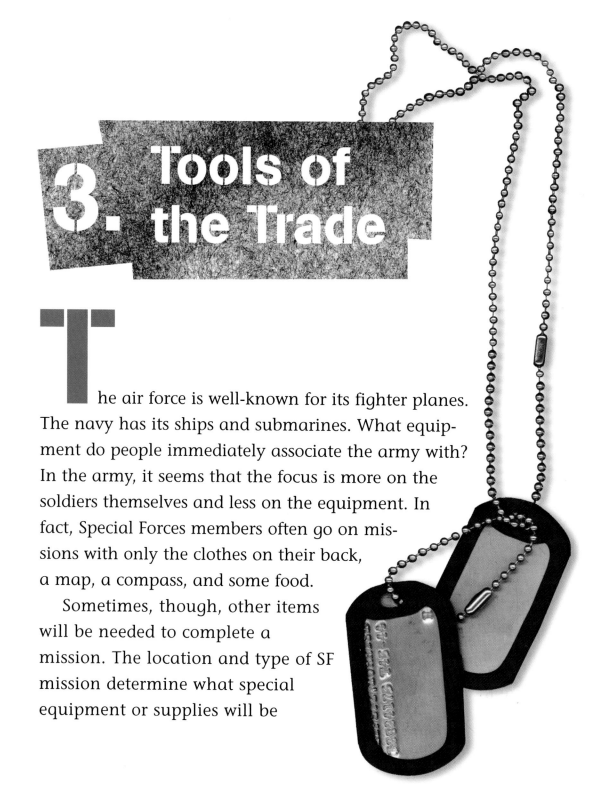

3. Tools of the Trade

The air force is well-known for its fighter planes. The navy has its ships and submarines. What equipment do people immediately associate the army with? In the army, it seems that the focus is more on the soldiers themselves and less on the equipment. In fact, Special Forces members often go on missions with only the clothes on their back, a map, a compass, and some food.

Sometimes, though, other items will be needed to complete a mission. The location and type of SF mission determine what special equipment or supplies will be needed. Depending on the type of mission, SF soldiers might not need anything but their skills and experience. For covert or clandestine operations, like a raid or a reconnaissance mission, an SF team may be able to take only the items that the members can carry in the packs on their backs. Sometimes, small loads can also be thrown to them from a helicopter or a cargo plane.

For a large-scale, overt mission, SF members will usually be able to get all the supplies and equipment they need. Humanitarian Assistance (HA) is an example of an overt mission. For an HA mission, very large loads can be flown into the area on a cargo plane. Large cargo planes, like the C-130 Hercules, can even carry the jeeps and trucks that SF members might need to move around in.

Clothing

The clothing worn by SF soldiers varies. It depends on both the weather at the mission site and on the type of mission.

Battle Dress Uniforms (BDUs) come in a variety of camouflage patterns. The woodland patterns are for areas covered with trees, bushes, and tall grass. The desert patterns are made to blend in with the sand and rocks. There are also urban patterns, meant to blend in with buildings,

In the mountain division, Special Forces soldiers must be outfitted in climate-appropriate gear, such as the Extended Cold Weather Clothing System (ECWCS).

shadows, and other things found in highly populated areas.

Soldiers working in cold-weather areas wear the Extended Cold Weather Clothing System (ECWCS). This system includes heavy pants and parkas designed to keep out cold and wetness. Helmets and flak jackets are used during firefights. New body armor is being developed that won't be as heavy to carry and wear.

Many SF missions require the members to become part of the culture of a foreign country. During these missions, they usually dress in the exact same types of clothes worn by the natives of that country.

Packs and Carriers

One thing that nearly every soldier wears is a rucksack (back-pack) to carry equipment and supplies. Since the mid-1970s, army soldiers have carried their loads in a rucksack known as ALICE. ALICE stands for All-Purpose Lightweight Individual Carrying Equipment. The ALICE system consists of a large pack with an aluminum frame and shoulder straps. The weight of the load sits on the soldier's shoulders and upper back.

Soldiers also carry a set of Load Bearing Gear known as the LC-2. This system was introduced in 1988. It looks like suspenders and a belt with different pouches and holders attached to it via hooks and clips. During a firefight, the ALICE pack can be dropped and cached so that the soldier can find it later. The LC-2 holds just what the soldier will need during the battle, including ammunition, grenades, a radio, a compass, and two canteens.

Using the ALICE and LC-2 systems, a soldier is expected to carry everything that will be needed for a three- to five-day mission in the field.

Over the years, soldiers have complained that the ALICE gear is big, heavy, and bulky. It is hard to carry on long marches since all the weight is on the back and shoulders. The U.S. Army Soldier Systems Center in Natick, Massachusetts, has developed

The much-improved MOLLE features a lightweight nylon mesh vest with removable pockets and a contoured plastic frame.

a new system to replace ALICE. It's called Modular Lightweight Load-Carrying Equipment, or MOLLE. The MOLLE system has many features that are big improvements over the ALICE system. The MOLLE frame is made out of a special lightweight plastic, instead of aluminum. The plastic stays strong in temperatures ranging from –40 degrees to 120 degrees Fahrenheit (-48 degrees to 49 degrees Celsius). During testing, many of the ALICE frames cracked after just one drop from an airplane. But the new MOLLE frames lasted five or more drops without damage.

The MOLLE system was also designed to be more comfortable for soldiers and to reduce fatigue. The weight of the MOLLE load rests between the shoulders and the hips instead of right on the shoulders. Soldiers can also transfer the weight to another part of their body if they get uncomfortable.

The LC-2 will also be replaced with a new system called the Fighting Load Carrier (FLC). The FLC is a vest instead of a belt. The weight is distributed evenly over the soldier's upper body. The LC-2 has metal clips and hooks that can sometimes dig into the skin. But the FLC uses pouches and pockets to hold ammunition, grenades, and canteens.

Food

Soldiers need to eat balanced meals to keep up their strength. During an overt mission, soldiers can cook and eat together at the base camp. But during a covert or clandestine mission, soldiers have to carry all their meals with them into the field. These meals have to be ready to eat, with no cooking required.

The army's standard field rations are called MREs. MRE is short for Meals Ready to Eat. They're packaged in a heavy plastic bag that has to be opened with a knife. Inside is a complete meal, including a main dish, a side dish like potatoes or rice, a drink, a dessert, and bread or a biscuit. There are over twenty-five varieties of MREs. The food stays fresh because it has been sterilized either by heat or radiation. Some of the ingredients are freeze-dried.

But there are many problems with MREs. One MRE weighs more than a pound, so carrying a few days' worth of meals can get very heavy. Some SF soldiers have learned how to save room and weight in their packs by opening the plastic bags before they head out on a mission. They take out the food they know they won't eat and they put the rest back into the bags. By doing this, they can sometimes carry as many as three meals in the same space they would have used for one.

Most MRE packs include an entrée, crackers and spread , a dessert, beverages, a plastic spoon, and a flameless heater. Although nutrition and taste are important, MREs must be extremely durable, in order to withstand rough handling and air drops. They must also be able to endure extreme weather and temperature ranges.

MREs also leave a lot of trash that soldiers must dispose of afterward. Many times, it is important for SF soldiers not to leave any evidence that they were in the area. So if their trash can't be buried, it must be carried along in the soldier's pack.

The army has several other meal options for soldiers. Some are used regularly, and some are still being researched and developed. Meal Cold Weather (MCW) and Long Range Patrol (LRP) rations are both completely freeze-dried. This makes them much lighter to carry, and they won't freeze in cold temperatures. However, MCWs and LRPs are both much more expensive than MREs, so the army uses them only when necessary, such as for missions in very cold weather.

Two types of Performance-Enhancing Ration Components (PERCs) have been introduced recently. The ERGO drink is a powder that's mixed with water to make a flavored beverage that contains vitamins and other nutrients. The HOOAH! Bar looks like a sports-nutrition bar, and it can easily be eaten on the run.

Mobility-Enhancing Ration Components (MERCs) are also becoming popular. MERCs are small, lightweight rations that look like a pocket pastry. They're filled with meat, cheese, vegetables, and lots of vitamins and nutrients. MERCs can also be eaten on the run.

Food is important, of course, but human beings could actually survive for days or even weeks without it if they had to. But no one can survive very long without fresh drinking water. SF soldiers need more than normal, too, since they are often working in very hot and dry areas. Their work can also be very stressful, which means they need even more water. Each soldier needs at least two gallons of water per day, and sometimes more.

At one time, canteens for carrying drinking water used to be very bulky and heavy. They were made of wood or heavy metals. But now they are made of lightweight plastic. The Camelbak Company developed a system to hydrate astronauts sealed in space suits. This type of system is now used by the army to hydrate their soldiers in the field.

The Camelbak system has a nylon bag with a plastic pouch inside. A plastic tube, like a long straw, leads from the pouch to the soldier's mouth. With this system, soldiers are able to drink without stopping, even while running. They do not have to stop and open a big, heavy canteen. One type of Camelbak unit is called Storm Maximum Gear. It was designed to be used with the new MOLLE system. Another unit is called the Stealth. It is for pilots and vehicle drivers. It fits between the wearer's back and the plane or vehicle seat so he can easily drink while flying or driving.

Weapons and Other Important Equipment

Many SF missions do not actually require the use of weapons. But the soldiers still have to be prepared for whatever happens during an operation. SF soldiers always carry weapons with them wherever they go. And all SF soldiers are fully trained to use all of the weapons available to them.

The soldier in the photo above is carrying an MG50 Squad Automatic Weapon, which is generally used in training. The inset shows an M16 rifle with scope.

The M16 rifle is considered one of the most important weapons for soldiers in the field. M16s are very light, weighing only about eight pounds. This makes carrying and handling them much easier than other weapons.

The standard light machine gun for the SF is the M249 Squad Automatic Weapon (SAW). It fires the same ammunition as the M16. The SAW can be hand-held or propped up with its built-in bipod, which is a two-legged stand.

Other weapons used by SF soldiers include pistols, hand grenades, grenade launchers, and land mines.

Most SF missions require that each soldier carry a map and a compass. But other necessary equipment depends on the type of mission. Night-vision goggles, radios, palm-sized computers, and digital cameras are all items that you might find packed in a soldier's rucksack.

Getting There

The final thing SF soldiers need is transportation to their designated area. The United States Transportation Command handles the job of getting the SF soldiers out of the United States and into the country where the mission will take place. From there, Air Force Special Operations will get the SF as close as possible to their intended target.

The hardest part, though, is getting SF troops to the mission's exact ground location. For overt operations, All-Terrain Vehicles (ATVs) and Ground Mobility Vehicles (GMVs) can be carried in on transport planes or helicopters. They can also be airdropped with parachutes. Once the vehicles are on the ground, they are used to move the troops and supplies from one location to another.

ATVs are lightweight, four-wheeled vehicles that can ride over rough ground. They can also tow small trailers filled

An SF soldier riding in an ATV catches up with soldiers on the side of a road in Afghanistan. ATVs and GMVs are essential forms of transportation for the Special Forces, especially in the rugged terrain of many enemy territories.

with extra supplies. GMVs were first used during the Persian Gulf War in Kuwait in the early 1990s. They look sort of like large sports utility vehicles, and heavy weapons can be mounted on them.

For covert or clandestine operations, SF soldiers must use the skills they learned during advanced parachute training. Being able to parachute within just a few feet of the mission's exact location is especially important.

4. The Special Forces in Action

It is only appropriate that the Green Berets should be part of our country's special forces. In every way, these individuals are truly special—specially selected, specially trained, specially equipped, and specially entrusted to successfully handle the most difficult missions. These missions break down into five main types.

Unconventional Warfare

The official motto of the SF is "De Oppresso Liber." In Latin, this means "To free the oppressed." Oppressed people are people whose freedom has been severely limited, usually by a group that has different

Green Berets don't spend all their time out in the field, gathering information and searching out the enemy. They also train in classrooms, strategize, and fill out paperwork. Above, a team is briefed before going out on a mission.

beliefs and ideals. This group has initiated some conflict to try to force their way of life, or their government, on others. Sometimes, the United States supports the government of the country where the conflict is taking place. Other times, the country itself is an enemy of the United States, and the United States supports the group that's trying to take over. SF members are following their motto when they practice unconventional warfare (UW).

UW is also called guerrilla warfare. As we learned earlier, guerrillas are non-soldiers who are trained to resist an enemy.

At the beginning of a UW mission, the A team moves into the target area to set up a camp. They fortify it with bunkers and trenches to protect themselves.

Next, they attempt to gain the trust of the people they were sent there to train. Sometimes, guerrilla groups are initially very hostile to the United States. They might not understand why or how the United States has come to help them. But the SF soldiers have learned the guerrillas' language and customs. This usually helps them gain the group's trust. Once the SF members have trained the guerrillas, they fight the enemy right alongside them.

Often, the guerrillas are trained soldiers who have already been fighting the enemy without the United States's help. In Afghanistan in 2001, SF teams were called in to help a guerrilla group that had already been fighting against the Taliban for more than ten years. The Taliban is a group of Islamic fundamentalists that forced very strict rules on the Afghan people. The guerrillas knew how to fight, but the SF educated them in other important ways on how to defeat the enemy. They taught them how to join together as one large group instead of trying to fight using lots of smaller, unorganized groups. They also instructed them in such things as

U.S. Special Forces work with Afghan special forces to search out Al Qaeda sympathizers following the September 11, 2001, terrorist attacks in the United States.

how to find good landing zones for their planes and good drop sites for their supplies.

Other times, though, the guerrillas may be ordinary citizens with no military training at all. In Vietnam in the 1960s, for instance, SF members trained villagers who lived high up in the mountains. They were training them to resist the Vietcong, a Communist group that was trying to take over the government of South Vietnam. South Vietnam was an ally of the United States, so the United States sent armed forces to help. The villagers had never seen the weapons that the United States brought with them. They were still using spears and crossbows for hunting and defense. But the United States military trained the guerrillas to use U.S. weapons to fight against the Vietcong. SF teams also patrolled the South Vietnamese borders to try to stop more Vietcong forces from getting in.

After the United States pulled out of Vietnam in 1974, many of the guerrillas the SF had trained joined the regular South Vietnamese army. But soon afterward, the Vietcong took over South Vietnam.

Foreign Internal Defense

Foreign Internal Defense (FID) missions are very similar to UW missions. However, FID missions usually take place during a time of peace instead of a time of war. And, instead of training guerrilla groups, SF teams train the actual military and police forces of an ally country. They prepare them for the possibility of the ally country being taken over by an enemy.

During both UW and FID missions, each of the SF team's specialists teaches his skills. The men share their knowledge of weapons, demolitions, communications, medicine, and espionage. SF teams often remain in the host country for six months or more while completing their mission.

Special Reconnaissance

Special Reconnaissance (SR) basically means spying on the enemy to get important information about them. SR might take place before a UW mission, when the SF needs to find out

On special reconnaissance missions, Green Berets may employ various methods, such as patrolling in the dark using night vision goggles, to obtain intelligence.

45

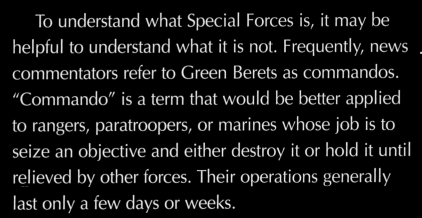

A Special Forces Member Shares His Memories

Staff Sergeant Gene Rice, Senior Intelligence Analyst 11th Special Forces Group (Airborne), 1965–1972

To understand what Special Forces is, it may be helpful to understand what it is not. Frequently, news commentators refer to Green Berets as commandos. "Commando" is a term that would be better applied to rangers, paratroopers, or marines whose job is to seize an objective and either destroy it or hold it until relieved by other forces. Their operations generally last only a few days or weeks.

The time frame for SF operations is not days or weeks, but months or years. Green Berets are recruited not only for their military skills, but for their teaching skills and their mind-set. What is sought is an unconventional approach to problem solving. Since the business is unconventional warfare, candidates need an unconventional thought process.

The A team is, essentially, a group of traveling school teachers. To equip them for this unusual role, they must learn the history, geography, language, religion, and culture of their operational area. That means that SF troops are not fully interchangeable. That means that the world has been divided into operational areas, and that we have people prepared to drop into any such area on very short notice.

During the period that I served, there was an enormous failure rate for candidates. It was said that for every 100 men who stepped forward and voiced an interest, only three survived the process and graduated. As for the physical torment, it was real. We were always either hot and dry or cold and wet. We were always hungry, thirsty, tired, and sore. Sometimes we were sick, sometimes we were injured, but we were always homesick and frequently terrified. I have a particular dislike for reptiles and lizards, and knowing that I was sleeping in their home did not improve my humor. But, to give a balanced view, there were good times as well.

What I remember more than anything else is, of course, the guys with whom I served. They were the most intelligent, articulate, dynamic, multitalented, and absolutely reliable group of men I have ever known. I would not say that I liked them all, but there was no one to whom I wouldn't give the last bit of water in my canteen.

Thinking back, dozens of pictures come to mind. I see a captain who visited us while we were firing mortars, a type of cannon. He told us not to get so used to sophisticated weapons that we forgot the simpler ones. We later learned that he knew this from experience. His camp in Vietnam had been overrun by the Vietcong. He lost his weapon and all he had to fight with was a small shovel, but he stopped nine Vietcong with it. He came to share his insights with us, because men in the SF are primarily teachers.

I remember a comrade who fought bravely. Before he was taken prisoner during World War II, he buried his tags and wallet so that he would not be identified as being Jewish. Since he had frostbitten feet, he was sent to work on the perimeter of the POW camp. He hit the guard with his shovel, hopped a fence, and jumped into an icy river. He managed to evade his pursuers and was picked up by some Italians. One hundred and one days later, he walked across American lines.

I learned more from men like these than from any class or exercise. I would not trade my time with them for any amount of money. Today, when so few young men want to enter the service, people seem impressed by my small contribution. What they do not grasp is that I was not making a sacrifice, I was gaining an invaluable education. For one brief period of time, I was able to walk with heroes, and my life was forever enriched.

more about the area where they will be setting up camp. If they are familiar with the terrain, weather, and wildlife, for instance, they will know which equipment and supplies to take with them.

SR can also take place during another mission. An SF team and its guerrillas can sneak up to an enemy camp and gain information for a future raid or bombing strike. It can gather information about the weapons the enemy is using or their plans against the United States and the guerrillas. SR can also happen following another mission. After bombs are dropped on an enemy area, an SF team will want to know whether the bombs hit their intended targets and how much of the enemy force is still alive.

Though SR missions require all of a team's members, the skills of the operations/intelligence specialists and communications specialists are especially important.

Counterterrorism

Counterterrorism (CT) involves training allies to resist terrorist activities. It can also involve taking direct action against a terrorist group. An SF team might need to gain more information about the terrorists, attack their base camps, or try to release hostages they have captured.

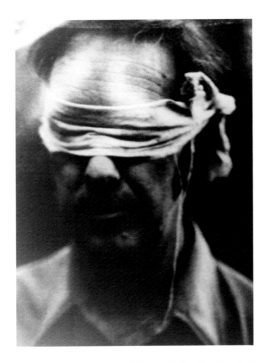

An attempt was made by a Special Forces counter-terrorism unit to rescue American hostages captured in Iran in 1979. Although the mission failed, the hostages were later released.

In April 1980, SF members took part in a CT mission to try to rescue forty-four American hostages held in Iran. These hostages had been captured at the U.S. Embassy in Tehran in 1979. The mission, called Operation Eagle Claw, was carried out by an SF team that had rescued prisoners during the Vietnam War. Operation Eagle Claw was one of the largest CT missions ever planned. Unfortunately, Operation Eagle Claw failed because of a sandstorm that forced many of the rescue aircraft to turn back. (The hostages were later released by their captors in January 1981.)

Five air force members and three marines were killed in Operation Eagle Claw. Dozens were injured.

Direct Action

SF teams can handle Direct Action (DA) missions, but Army Rangers are often called in to handle them instead. A DA mission involves a very quick strike against an enemy target. It could come in the form of a raid, a sabotage effort, an ambush, or a bombing. The purpose of a DA is to capture, disable, or destroy a target. With the help of the communications specialists and the weapons specialists, weapons can be directed at the targets from gunships and bombers in the sky overhead.

During Operation Enduring Freedom in 2001 and 2002, SF teams and Army Rangers performed many DA missions in Afghanistan. They were searching caves and mountainsides for terrorist leader Osama bin Laden. Whenever a Taliban or Al Qaeda hideout was discovered, the area would either be raided or bombed by the soldiers. Taliban or Al Qaeda buildings and equipment left behind would also be destroyed or sabotaged.

Besides these five missions, there are many other types of missions that SF teams are often called upon to handle:

Combat Search and Rescue

The purpose of a Combat Search and Rescue (CSAR) mission is to rescue military personnel. If a group of soldiers in enemy

Green Berets provide humanitarian relief around the world. Here, a soldier helps evacuate children from warring Liberia to safety in Senegal.

territory is being overpowered, they must be rescued before they are captured. Or a military aircraft may have crashed or been shot down, and the crews must be rescued from deep within enemy territory.

Humanitarian Assistance

During Humanitarian Assistance (HA) missions, SF members provide relief for large masses of people. This includes people who have been affected by a huge natural disaster, like an earthquake. Medical specialists can help care for the injured people, while other SF team members set up camps and kitchens.

HA missions also help refugees. These are people who are fleeing their country because of the violence there. Refugees need help getting to a safe place and finding food and shelter. In December 2001, the SF helped more than 100,000 refugees in Afghanistan. The refugees were stranded in Bamiyan, a city high up in the mountains. The only access to Bamiyan is a dirt road over a mountain pass, and winter snow had blocked the road. By using the C-130 Hercules cargo plane, SF members were able to get food, blankets, and medical supplies to the refugees.

Peacekeeping

When a war or other conflict has ended in a foreign country, SF members often stay there to help make sure that the problems don't start again and that all involved are adhering to the terms of any peace agreements.

The Future of Special Forces: What Will Tomorrow Bring?

When enrollment levels for all of the military's branches are down, the Special Forces are affected, too. If fewer people are joining the military, then there are fewer men who can qualify to become SF members.

Some people have suggested making the Q Course a little bit easier so that more men would be able to pass it. But military experts believe that this would do more harm than good. They don't want SF members out in the field who aren't skilled and highly trained. To do this would be to risk injury or death to the members of the SF team. When the army opened up SF recruiting to non-soldiers in 2001, they gave themselves more candidates to choose from. But the new candidates have to meet even stricter qualifications than existing soldiers do. Opening up recruitment did not weaken the system, but making the Q Course easier definitely would.

Another idea is to reduce the number of A teams in each SF company. There are currently six A teams per company. But if that number could be reduced to three or four teams, it would make all of the A teams stronger. Each team would be made up of only the most skilled SF members from all the teams.

There was a time, not too many years ago, when military experts wondered whether SF teams would always be needed.

Though military conflicts were still present in parts of the world, there also seemed to be more peace than ever before.

After the terrorist attacks on the United States on September 11, 2001, such doubts were put to rest. Our military now realizes that their defense tactics and peacekeeping skills will probably always be needed. As long as there are people in the world, there will be conflicts that need to be resolved. And as long as there is fighting, the Special Forces will be needed to carry out their very special missions. There will be new and difficult challenges to face all the time. But with help from advances in technology, these special individuals will always have new and improved tools and equipment to accomplish their goals. And with the proven dedication and determination of the SF, there is no group better trained and prepared to handle those challenges, both at home and all over the world.

Glossary

battalion   A military unit that is part of a larger unit.

bunker   An underground shelter.

cache   To hide something, such as food, equipment, or supplies, often underground.

camouflage   The disguising of soldiers or vehicles so that they blend in with their surroundings, making it harder for them to be seen by their enemies.

clandestine   Done in secret.

classified   Secret or restricted.

Communism   A political system based on the public ownership of all property.

covert   Not openly practiced.

detachment   A group of military troops on a special assignment.

espionage The art or practice of spying.

fatigue Extreme tiredness.

flak jacket A bulletproof jacket or vest, worn to protect soldiers from gunfire.

fluent Able to write or speak easily in a foreign language.

fortify To make stronger, or to provide with military defense.

freeze-dried Food that is preserved by being frozen quickly, then dried in a high vacuum.

guerrilla A member of a small military band that uses stealth and terrorist tactics to attack a larger group or government.

navigate To control the course of a person or vehicle.

overt Open and visible, not secret.

sabotage The destruction of property or equipment, done intentionally.

sterilize To destroy bacteria and germs.

triage Sorting injured people and treating them based on their need for medical treatment.

For More Information

In the United States

U.S. Army Public Affairs

1500 Army Pentagon
Washington, DC 20310-1500
(703) 697-4314
Web site: http://www.dtic.mil/armylink

U.S. Special Forces

Fort Bragg, NC 28307
(910) 396-0111
Web site: http://www.specialforces.net

In Canada

Department of National Defence

National Defence Headquarters

Major-General George R. Pearkes Building

101 Colonel By Drive

Ottawa, ON K1A 0K2

(613) 995-2534

Web site: http://www.dnd.ca

Royal Military College of Canada

P.O. Box 17000 Stn Forces

Kingston, ON K7K 7B4

(613) 541-6000

Web site: http://www.rmc.ca

Web Sites

Due to the changing nature of Internet links, the Rosen Publishing Group, Inc., has developed an online list of Web sites related to the subject of this book. This site is updated regularly. Please use this link to access the list:

http://www.rosenlinks.com/iso/grbe

For Further Reading

Miller, David. *Modern Elite Forces*. New York: Smithmark
Publishers, 1992.

Moran, Tom. *The U.S. Army*. Minneapolis, MN: Lerner
Publications, 1990.

Paradis, Adrian A. *Opportunities in Military Careers*. Chicago:
NTC/Contemporary Publishing Group, 1999.

Streissguth, Tom. *The Green Berets*. Mankato, MN: Capstone
Press, 1996.

The Visual Dictionary of Special Military Forces. New York:
Dorling Kindersley, Inc., 1993.

Walner, Max. *An Illustrated Guide to Modern Elite Forces*. New
York: Arco, 1984.

Bibliography

Clancy, Tom. *Special Forces*. New York: Berkley Publishing
   Group, 2001.

Green, Michael. *The United States Army*. Mankato, MN:
   Capstone Press, 1998.

Halberstadt, Hans. *Green Berets: Unconventional Warriors*.
   Novato, CA: Presidio Press, 1988.

Hassig, Lee E., et al., eds. *Special Forces and Special Missions*.
   Alexandria, VA: Time-Life Books, 1990.

Paradis, Adrian A. *Opportunities in Military Careers*. Chicago:
   NTC/Contemporary Publishing Group, 1999.

Simons, Anna. *The Company They Keep: Life Inside the U.S. Army
   Special Forces*. New York: The Free Press, 1997.

Simpson, Charles M., III. *Inside the Green Berets: The First Thirty
   Years*. Novato, CA: Presidio Press, 1983.

Streissguth, Tom. *The Green Berets*. Mankato, MN: Capstone
   Press, 1996.

Index

About the Author

Jan Goldberg is an experienced, credentialed educator and the author of forty-five nonfiction books, hundreds of educational articles, textbooks, and other projects.

Credits

Cover, pp. 1, 18, 32, 34, 37, 41 © Hans Halberstadt/Military Stock Photo; p. 4 © Reuters NewMedia Inc./Corbis; pp. 9, 13, 39, 42, 52 © AP/Wide World Photos; p. 12 © Patrick Baz/Reuters/Timepix; p. 21 © Corbis; pp. 26, 30 © Greg Mathieson/MAI/Timepix; p. 27 © SSG Glynn/US Army/Timepix; p. 45 © Leif Skoogfors/Corbis; p. 50 © Bettmann/Corbis.

Editor

Christine Poolos

Design and Layout

Les Kanturek